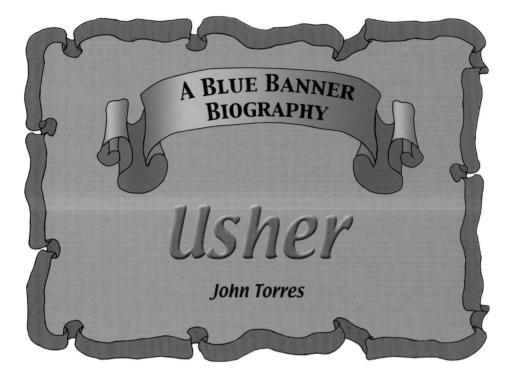

A BLUE BANNER
BIOGRAPHY

Usher

John Torres

P.O. Box 196
Hockessin, Delaware 19707
Visit us on the web: www.mitchelllane.com
Comments? email us: mitchelllane@mitchelllane.com

Mitchell Lane PUBLISHERS

Printing   4   5   6   7   8   9

Blue Banner Biographies

Alan Jackson	Alicia Keys	Allen Iverson
Ashanti	Ashlee Simpson	Ashton Kutcher
Avril Lavigne	Bernie Mac	Beyoncé
Bow Wow	Britney Spears	Carrie Underwood
Chris Brown	Christina Aguilera	Christopher Paul Curtis
Ciara	Clay Aiken	Condoleezza Rice
Daniel Radcliffe	David Ortiz	Derek Jeter
Eminem	Eve	Fergie (Stacy Ferguson)
50 Cent	Gwen Stefani	Ice Cube
Jamie Foxx	Ja Rule	Jay-Z
Jennifer Lopez	Jessica Simpson	J. K. Rowling
Jodie Foster	Johnny Depp	JoJo
Justin Berfield	Justin Timberlake	Kate Hudson
Keith Urban	Kelly Clarkson	Kenny Chesney
Lance Armstrong	Lindsay Lohan	Mariah Carey
Mario	Mary J. Blige	Mary-Kate and Ashley Olsen
Michael Jackson	Miguel Tejada	Missy Elliott
Nancy Pelosi	Nelly	Orlando Bloom
P. Diddy	Paris Hilton	Peyton Manning
Queen Latifah	Ron Howard	Rudy Giuliani
Sally Field	Selena	Shakira
Shirley Temple	Tim McGraw	**Usher**
Zach Efron		

Library of Congress Cataloging-in-Publication Data
Torres, John Albert.
    Usher / By John Torres.
       p. cm. — (A blue banner biography)
    Includes discography (p.), bibliographical references (p.), and index.
    ISBN 1-58415-379-2 (library bound)
       1. Usher—Juvenile literature. 2. Singers—United States—Biography—Juvenile literature.
I. Title. II. Series.
ML3930.U84T67 2005
782.421643'092—dc22
                                                      2004030259
ISBN-13: 9781584153795

ABOUT THE AUTHOR: John A. Torres is an award-winning journalist covering social issues for *Florida Today Newspaper*. John has also written more than 25 books for various publishers on a variety of topics. He wrote *P. Diddy, Mia Hamm,* and *The Disaster in the Indian Ocean, Tsunami 2004* for Mitchell Lane Publishers. In his spare time John likes playing sports, going to theme parks, and fishing with his children, step-children, and wife, Jennifer.

PHOTO CREDITS: Cover, p. 27—Vince Bucci/Getty Images; pp. 4, 8, 11, 20, 21—Frank Micelotta/ Getty Images; p. 10—Lisa Rose/Globe Photos; p. 16—Kevin Mazur/WireImage; p. 17—Jamie Kondrchek; p. 22—Robin Platzer/Twin Images/Getty Images; p. 25—Dave Hogan/Getty Images; p. 26—Paul Warner/AP Photo; p. 28—Rick Diamond.

PLB2,29,30

CONTENTS

Usher, known for his hip clothes and his sense of style, is also known for his strong presence on stage. Here, he strikes a pose during a concert in Puerto Rico in March 2005, before giving the fans what they want: more Usher!

Crossroads

You can't really blame Usher for being so confident. After all, when you're in your twenties and have already won a string of Grammy Awards, have sold millions of copies of your music albums, are set to star in a major movie, and are known to be one of the most beautiful people in the world, it can be hard to stay humble.

He's also heard the comparisons. People say that Usher sings like such legendary singers as Frank Sinatra, Michael Jackson, Luther Vandross, and Marvin Gaye. They also say that he dances like Michael Jackson and Fred Astaire. It can be too much for a young man to hear. But not for Usher.

"I'm the greatest of my time," Usher joked during an interview. "I'm a living legend. I'm the prettiest. I don't care what nobody says."

But then he laughs and credits his mother for teaching him to work very hard, to believe in himself, to have confidence—but also to stay grounded and to stay humble.

Perhaps his mother's influence and his upbringing helped Usher Raymond reach his musical success. He may have been relying on her wisdom again to help him through the next major crossroads in his career.

Having started as a teenage pop music sensation, Usher transformed himself into a successful rhythm and blues singer. He then remade himself again and put himself on top of the hip-hop music world. It seems as if he is able to sing and be successful in any popular music form.

But even these accomplishments have not been enough for the rich-voiced singer and dancer who sells out concert halls all over the country. He tells people that his dream is to become an all-around complete entertainer.

That is why Usher was tackling motion pictures as his next challenge. The key has been not to lose the fans of his music, and not to forget that it was music that made him so popular to begin with. Moving into movies has also

> *Having started as a teenage pop music sensation, Usher transformed himself into a successful rhythm and blues singer.*

been a gamble because Usher had to fight hard to gain control of the music he records. By 2004 he had finally established his own "Usher Sound." Branching out could have put his music in jeopardy.

In fact, Usher mentioned that he was taking cues from one of his mentors, or teachers, Sean "P. Diddy" Combs. P. Diddy, a rapper, branched out and became successful in several areas, including acting, designing his own clothing line, owning restaurants, and, of course, singing.

"I'm not a follower but I do follow greatness," Usher said. "There's nothing wrong with recognizing greatness from the past and mimicking it to create something great for the future."

As 2004 drew to a close, Usher sat back and enjoyed the success of his latest album, *Confessions*, and the fact that the song "Yeah" was one of the biggest singles of the year on several music charts. He had worked hard to make appearances and do a promotional concert tour for the album. He practiced his dance moves daily and was constantly trying to make his songwriting better and keep his singing voice fluid and smooth.

That's why he gets angry when people criticize him. Some say his path has been easy or that he is too

"I'm not a follower but I do follow greatness," Usher said. "There's nothing wrong with recognizing greatness . . . and mimicking it . . ."

confident, too cocky. Usher believes he has worked too hard to let people try to knock him down.

"I hear people say, 'He's a little too confident,'" Usher said with a frown. "Well, I mean, wouldn't you be if nobody believed in your dreams but you? I don't speak arrogantly. I speak confidently."

That confidence did not come after Usher made it to the top of the charts. It began many years before, when he was singing in a small church choir in Tennessee.

Usher is not afraid to show how proud he is of his CD, Confessions, *at a signing at the Virgin Megastore in New York City. The recording has sold more than 9 million copies around the world.*

Childhood Dreams

Usher Raymond was born on October 14, 1978, in Chattanooga, Tennessee. Like many modern hip-hop superstars, Usher was brought up mainly by his mother. His father had moved out of the home when Usher was very young.

After a while, Usher saw less and less of his real father.

"I did have a dad, if you get me," Usher said. "But not a real father." He also commented, "I didn't really have a dad. I didn't have that energy to pull from."

Lucky for Usher that his mother, Jonnetta Patton, had plenty of energy to draw from. She also opened a world in which Usher could find his own energy: music. Jonnetta was the choir director for St. Elmo's Missionary Baptist Church.

While his mother liked music, Usher loved sports. He dreamed of becoming a basketball or football player. But he was always a bit small for his age. Even today, as an

Usher, who credits his mother Jonneta with helping him develop his musical talent and becoming a star, gives her a kiss on the cheek for the cameras on the red carpet outside the 41st Annual Grammy Awards.

adult, he is only five feet nine and a half inches tall. He never felt he was big enough to be good at playing sports.

Instead, he started to sing. He joined his mother's church choir and learned how to sing hymnals and gospel music. Once he was exposed to the music in church, Usher started noticing music everywhere.

He sometimes jokes that while growing up in a sleepy Southern town, there wasn't much to do except listen to music. After his musical education began, it went straight from church to his grandmother's house. There the blues were always coming from her record player. Usher learned the classic bluesy sounds and started listening to some of the masters.

He didn't always know that he could make a career out of his love for music. He told his grandmother once

It's clear that good looks run in the family. Here Usher celebrates his Grammy successes with his brother James at a private party hosted by Entertainment Weekly.

that his dream was to save enough money to open a Krispy Kreme doughnut shop.

Usher's mother loved to listen to soul music. Her favorite singer was Marvin Gaye, who influenced generations of music lovers with his soulful, caring voice. He sang about things like injustice and social issues. One album in particular influenced Usher and made him want to become a singer.

"Marvin Gaye's *What's Going On* stands as one of the best albums I've ever heard," said Usher.

During this time, Usher was not such a great student in school. He couldn't really focus on the things he needed to in order to be successful there. His mother later explained that maybe it was because there were so many creative thoughts going on in Usher's head that school just maybe wasn't for him.

Usher would go around the house singing. Performing in the choir also helped him overcome any shyness he may have had about singing in public. His mother encouraged him to sing and perform all the time. She felt, even when he was young, that her son had a chance to make it big. She started enrolling him in singing competitions throughout the South.

"I have been building my career since I was a little boy because singing had always been what I wanted to do," Usher said. "At first I thought about playing football and then I wanted to play basketball, but in the end it was all about the music. It's my biggest passion and my biggest joy."

There was one particular childhood event that really convinced Usher that music was what he should do with the rest of his life.

He went with his aunt to see New Edition in concert.

Early Training

*I*n the 1980s, pop music was being influenced more and more by rhythm and blues. That was one of the reasons Usher wanted to see the popular band New Edition in concert. But it wasn't only their music. He also admired their dance moves and just how cool the group looked when the members sang and danced as one.

It was the first time he had ever been to a big-time pop concert. Even though he and his aunt had seats very far away from the stage, Usher had the time of his life. The concert would change him forever.

"I remember the choreography, I remember the lights, I remember the crowd screaming and the excitement," he said. "I had a horrible seat, but that was one of the highlights of my life, man. It was one of the things that made me want to do this."

He had the bug. Usher was convinced, even as a preteen, that he would find happiness — as well as fame and fortune—as a performer. He began studying Michael Jackson performances on television and practicing his moves as well as his singing. He couldn't get enough of watching how other singers and dancers performed. It proved to be very valuable training. Soon Usher had a series of dance moves that he had come up with all on his own. He was always very limber and energetic. He could do things on the dance floor that others couldn't do.

Usher's mother really began taking an interest in her son's new hobby, and she decided to get actively involved.

Usher's mother really began taking an interest in her son's new hobby, and she decided to get actively involved. She found out that a teen boy-band was forming in Chattanooga that would be singing rhythm and blues. Usher tried out for the group and soon was the star of the ensemble.

Not only did Usher have a great singing voice and terrific dance moves, but he also had the look. He was, and still is, very handsome. He had the face of a pop star.

The group started playing at local talent shows and in mini-concerts. Even though the group was well received and fans seemed to like their music and their moves, after two years they were no closer to stardom than when they first started.

Usher's mother decided to take a chance and make a major move. Because she believed so strongly in her son's talent, she decided they would leave their home and move to Atlanta, Georgia. Atlanta had become a hotbed of musical talent. If Usher was going to be discovered and become famous, it was more likely to happen there than in Chattanooga, Tennessee.

When they got to Atlanta, Usher wasn't intimidated at all. He was full of charisma and had a desire to succeed. He began playing talent shows. Then he heard that *Star Search* was holding auditions for their television show. It was 1991, and he was thirteen years old.

Usher was so close now, he could taste it. Others around him could see as well that desire in him to succeed.

Frank Gatson Jr., an entertainment executive and a choreographer for more than twenty years, said that Usher "saw himself [as a star] from the time he was on *Star Search*."

Later, Gatson would get to work with Usher as a creative adviser.

Usher sang and danced his heart out on *Star Search*. Though he didn't win the contest, there were a few

Usher's mother decided to take a chance and make a major move . . . to Atlanta, Georgia. Atlanta had become a hotbed of musical talent.

people in the audience who noticed how talented this young teenager was.

Those talent scouts spoke to the young man and his mother about an audition with Antonio "L.A." Reid. A cofounder of LaFace Records, Reid was a very famous

Usher has never forgotten the people that helped him along when his career was just getting off the ground. Here he celebrates with Antonio "L.A." Reid, who offered Usher his very first record deal.

producer in the rhythm and blues world. Usher would then meet with Kenneth "Babyface" Edmonds, who was Reid's partner and a music superstar in his own right.

Reid and Edmonds thought Usher sounded great and had what it took. When Usher was fourteen, they offered him a record deal. Usher was on his way to musical superstardom. But his path wouldn't be without obstacles.

Just as quickly as he became a pop sensation, Usher also became a sex symbol. He is very comfortable around the camera: something his fans love.

Meeting his Mentor

*E*ven before the ink was dry on his brand-new
recording contract, Usher began going through puberty.
Puberty is the time when a child changes into an adult.
One of the things that changes is the child's voice. For a
boy it becomes deeper, sometimes raspy. It can switch
back and forth between high and low before it settles on a
tone. It can squeak without warning.

For Usher, the voice changes were nearly disastrous.
His singing career was almost over before it started. After
all, the music executives at LaFace Records were
interested in the child star with the sweet young voice.
Now his voice was changing, and production on Usher's
first recording had to be delayed.

It was a terrible time for the kid from Chattanooga
who did not have much patience. He wanted to get into
the studio and show that he could become a superstar.

"I couldn't stop it," he said of his voice changing. "And, I couldn't speed it up."

By this time, Usher had been sent to New York City, where he would be recording with Sean "Puff Daddy" Combs. (Combs is now known as P. Diddy.) The two put their heads together and decided to hire a voice coach. This training was very important, because once the transformation was complete, Usher basically had to relearn how to sing.

It worked. And Usher sounded better than ever.

Another hardship during this time was that Usher was living in New York City without his mother. Combs was known for being big into parties and the New York nightlife. Would Usher be able to handle the temptations that a city like New York can offer a teenager living on his own?

Usher enjoyed his time in New York. Even though sometimes things got a little wild, he was able to maintain who he was and stay out of trouble.

> Usher enjoyed his time in New York. Even though sometimes things got a little wild, he was able to maintain who he was and stay out of trouble.

"My mother wasn't there, and I saw a lot—an awful lot—of things in New York City," he said. "But I didn't soak up the bad things because my mother didn't raise me to be weak-minded."

Finally, in 1994, Usher's first album, *Usher*, was released. The record got decent radio play and eventually sold a million copies. Some of the critics, though, thought the material was too risqué for a fourteen-year-old to be singing.

Usher toured and sang at clubs to promote the record. Meanwhile he continued to live with Combs; he viewed Combs as his mentor. Soon the two got back into the studio to find the exact sound that they wanted to sell.

Usher was groomed for stardom by many people, including Sean "P. Diddy" Combs. Usher actually lived with Combs while he was learning the ropes of the music business. Here the duo share the stage during an October 13, 2004, concert at New York's Madison Square Garden.

The idea was to soften the sound a bit and get back to Usher's rhythm and blues roots. They also might have him sing more romantic ballads instead of dance songs with heavy sexual overtones.

P. Diddy worked on the record, but there was additional help this time. Jermaine Dupri, who was well known in the Atlanta music world, produced seven tracks on the record. Edmonds supplied some ballads as well. The hard work took nearly three years, but when it was finally released, *My Way* was regarded as a masterpiece.

The record went platinum, meaning it sold a million copies. It also earned the singer his first Grammy

Usher is always at the center of attention. He poses with record producer Jermaine Dupri and legendary singer Janet Jackson at the world premier of the concert film Jay-Z Fade to Black.

nomination. That's when people outside the music industry began noticing how talented and appealing Usher was. They began signing him to appear on television. He landed recurring roles on the UPN show *Moesha* and on the soap opera *The Bold and the Beautiful*. Usher loved being on screen. He soon set his sights on being in the movies as well. One of his first movie roles was in the movie *The Faculty*.

"You can't plan it," he said about his success. "I can't say that I expected that type of success, but I was given the opportunity. Of course that was only the beginning."

Usher's music and entertainment careers were well on their way. All that was left was superstardom. But would it be that easy?

Like many pop stars, Usher aspires to becoming a movie star as well. Usher appears in the movie The Faculty. *The cast members from left to right are Jordana Brewster, Shawn Hatosy, Usher Raymond, Clea Duvall, Josh Hartnett, and Elijah Wood.*

Superstar

*U*sher's second album contained something that his first recording did not: a smash hit single. The song "You Make Me Wanna" made it to number two on the pop charts and number one on the rhythm and blues (R&B) singles charts.

Based on his newfound popularity, Usher was asked to tour with and be the opening act for such legendary artists as Janet Jackson and Mary J. Blige. He also made the cover of the magazines *Vibe* and *Teen People*.

In 1999, the Usher *Live* album was released. It would give a concert album to fans who weren't lucky enough to hear him sing in person. And for fans who were, it would let them relive the thrill of seeing him on stage.

During all this success, Usher still kept his mother as his manager. The two share a very unique relationship. It sometimes centers only on business and other times on family. In appreciation, Usher bought his mother a beautiful four-story house just outside Atlanta.

Even though Usher was making television appearances and touring throughout the country, his fans were begging for more new music from the singing sensation. He soon returned to the studio to record *8701*. (The title *8701* comes from the album's release date: August 7, 2001.) It sold an incredible eight million copies. He won his second Grammy Award, this time for best R&B performance for "U Remind Me."

For his next album, Usher was once again teamed with the talented producer Jermaine Dupri. The producer would talk to Usher for hours about the kind of music they wanted to make and what sort of range and sound Usher's voice could handle. Usher credits Dupri with giving him the confidence to be successful and to take more chances on his fourth studio recording, *Confessions*, released in March 2004. Afterward, Usher paid Dupri a great compliment.

"I would compare it to the great combination of Michael Jackson and Quincy Jones," Usher said. "Certain producers just naturally understand how to make great music for you and I think that Jermaine Dupri is one of those people."

On *Confessions*, Usher decided to write many of the songs himself. It is rumored to be a very personal album dealing with his breakup with a girlfriend. The fans loved

> *Even though Usher was making television appearances and touring throughout the country, his fans were begging for more new music. . . .*

In what many saw as a "changing of the guard," pop legend Michael Jackson shares the stage with the man expected to take over as the next "King of Pop," Usher. This was taken at a 2001 concert in New York's Madison Square Garden.

it; they also loved Usher's songwriting style. *Confessions* was *Billboard*'s number one album of 2004, and "Yeah!" was the chart's hottest single of the year.

For Usher, it was a logical next step in his career to start having more control over his material.

"Once I figured out the formula, I said 'You know what? Who's going to write a better song for me than myself?' " he said. "The more comfortable I felt with speaking about my personal life and personal situations, I began to do it. People helped me articulate myself. Then I got to a point where I felt like I could do it myself."

Besides becoming a music superstar, Usher also was able to do something that not many before him had accomplished. He made the transition from a teen singing sensation to an adult superstar and sex symbol.

Not only is Usher a star, he is also known for his generosity and love of children. He contributes to The Rainbow Connection, an organization that works to fulfill the wishes of dying children with life-threatening diseases, and he is known to appear at Read to Achieve celebrations.

During one stretch of 2004, Usher also made musical history when he had three songs—"Yeah," "Burn," and "Confessions, Pt. II,"—all in the *Billboard* Top Ten at the same time. The only other performers to ever accomplish that were the Beatles and the Bee Gees. He's had so many

Usher is more than just a pop star whose fans swoon over him. He is also a caring individual who is involved in many charities. Here, he makes a dying girl's wish come true. This photo was taken on February 21, 1999. Usher visits with 7-year-old Jasmine Rowe. Usher found out through The Rainbow Connection that the girl's wish before she died was to meet him and have him sing to her.

Usher promotes reading during a courtside show during the NBA 2003 All-Star weekend. The event was aimed at trying to get some of Usher's younger fans — or basketball fans in general — to continue reading.

songs make it to the top spot on the charts that in Europe he's known as Mr. One-derful.

Fans will be happy to learn that Usher has absolutely no plans of slowing down. In fact, he could soon be busier than ever. After playing the legendary soul singer Jackie Wilson in the 2004 movie *Ray*, he thought making a movie about Wilson should be his next step. Usher would not only be starring as the singer, but would also be producing the film.

It is all part of Usher's grand plan to succeed in every facet of the entertainment world.

"As a stage performer, I feel like I'm at the top of my game," he said. "But being an ultimate entertainer is not just about being a stage performer. It's about being an actor, a producer, a director. I'm getting closer and closer every day. Hopefully one day I'll win an Oscar for a video or a short film. Maybe I'll go on Broadway; maybe I'll produce an album on a solo artist or group."

With Usher's track record so far, he may be able to accomplish all that and more.

The late, great Ray Charles, accepts the Atlanta Heroes Award from Usher, who later appeared in the movie about the late singer's life as singer/ performer Jackie Wilson.

CHRONOLOGY

1978	Usher Raymond is born in Chattanooga, Tennessee, on October 14.
1990	Usher, his mother, and his younger brother move to Atlanta.
1991	Usher is spotted by a talent scout from LaFace while he is performing on *Star Search*; a record contract soon follows.
1993	Usher's debut LaFace single, "Call Me a Mack," makes the R&B chart.
1994	*Usher* is released.
1997	"You Make Me Wanna" hits number one in R&B in its second week out; *My Way* is released. Usher receives his first Grammy nomination for Best Male R&B Vocal Performance for "You Make Me Wanna"; the song is also nominated for a Soul Train Music Award for Best Male R&B/Soul Single.
1997	Usher is cast in the family TV series *Moesha*.
1998	Usher has his first lead role in a movie, the thriller *The Faculty*. He is also cast in the daytime drama *The Bold and the Beautiful*.
1999	Usher completes two more films, *She's All That* and *Light It Up*. He begins community activities as a role model to youth.
2004	By Thanksgiving, Usher has a yearly total of 28 weeks at number one on the Billboard charts. He is the only artist in history ever to top the Hot 100 for more than half a year. *Confessions* is named Billboard's number one album, and "Yeah!" is the chart's hottest single of year.
2005	Usher wins three Grammys, four Soul Train Music Awards, and an NRJ Music Award for International Male Artist of the Year. He produces his first movie, *In the Mix*.
2006	He organizes *Usher's New Look*, his philanthropic organization for teens; appears on Broadway in *Chicago*.
2007	Usher wins NAACP Spirit Award.

DISCOGRAPHY

2005	*Usher Presents In the Mix* (sound track)
2004	*Confessions*
2001	*8701*
1999	*Live*
1997	*My Way*
1994	*Usher*

FILMOGRAPHY

2005	*In the Mix* (is also executive producer)
2004	*Ray* (cameo as Jackie Wilson)
2001	*Texas Rangers*
2000	*Geppetto* (TV movie)
1999	*Light It Up*
1999	*She's All That*
1998	*The Bold and the Beautiful* (TV Series)
1998	*The Faculty*
1997–1999	*Moesha* (TV Series)

FOR FURTHER READING

Bronson, Fred. The Billboard 200: "Usher Takes the Cake." http://www.billboard.com/bb/yearend/2004/bb200.jsp

Christensen, Thor. "How Usher Stays on Top," *Monterey County Herald*, August 17, 2004, Life Section (Knight Ridder Newspapers).

Duerden, Nick. "King of Bling," *The London Independent*, May 29, 2004, Features Section.

Foege, Alec. "Pop Music," *The Los Angeles Times*, August 5, 2001, Calendar.

Jones, Steve. "A Seasoned Usher Aims Even Higher," *USA Today*, March 23, 2004.

Spera, Keith. "Usher on Top," *New Orleans Times-Picayune*, August 13, 2004.

Venable, Malcolm. "All Hail Usher," *The Virginian-Pilot*, August 5, 2004.

On the Internet

UsherWorld: The Official Website of Usher
http://www.usherworld.com/
MTV.com – Usher
www.mtv.com/bands/az/usher/artist.jhtml
Arista Records: Usher
www.aristarec.com/aristaweb/Usher

INDEX